To my little brother, Kion.

Written by Faith Cellan
Edited by Jamie C. McHugh
Illustrated by Raven Moonfall

An axolotl named Archer lived in Lake Xochimilco in Mexico. He is a little unique. He has a long, slimy tail and huge, fluffy gills. Even more unusual, he is able to rebuild his limbs.

When he was a young larva being chased by bullies, Archer accidentally damaged his tail on sharp rocks. It was painful for him, but his tail grew back as if nothing had happened.

Archer's parents deeply loved him. Unfortunately, they are endangered and there were few axolotls left in Lake Xochimilco. This made Archer and his family feel unwelcome. As there are not many like them, they got picked on a lot.

Other fish frequently bullied Archer's parents too. They would laugh, whisper behind their backs, and try to avoid them, even if they were nice. Life was lonely for Archer and his family.

At school, the other fish ridiculed Archer for his unique appearance and abilities. Dan Danio and Georgia Gourami, his closest friends, never stopped supporting and defending him from bullies.

He endured insults like 'weirdo,' 'alien,' and 'freak' on a daily basis. It was difficult for Archer to ignore the bullying. Concentrating on his schoolwork soon became very challenging. Often, he'd lose interest and not want to attend school due to his loneliness.

One day, a group of predators entered their lake searching for prey. It was complete chaos at Lake Xochimilco.

Since many of the fish had been injured, Archer felt he needed to act fast before things worsened. He was very terrified, but he knew someone had to do something to stop the predators.

He stood strong and ordered the predators to leave. Archer's attempt to be a hero resulted in a brutal attack. The fight against the invaders injured his fins and tail. They even made fun of him as he lay helpless.

While he was down, Archer remembered the time he injured himself when he was still a larva. He recalled how special he was. He used his ability for regeneration to build brand-new fins and a tail.

Archer displayed bravery, for sure. But he wasn't a fighter. Despite his unique ability to rebuild his limbs, he still could not defeat the invaders. There were too many of them.

The predators damaged Archer's community. Homes were destroyed. Everyone was hurt, and his friends, Dan, and Georgia, were severely injured. Before the predators left, they threatened everyone that they would be back to cause more damage.

Weeks went by, and everyone fully recovered from their injuries. While most fish were trying to rebuild their homes, some chose to move far away because of the threat of another predator attack. Archer's family and closest friends decided to stay, but they had to be alert all the time.

A few weeks went by, and everything felt normal. Archer was again getting bullied in school. Nothing much had changed.

One day, Archer, Dan, and Georgia were on their way home from class. They came across an elderly Siamese fighting fish who had recently moved into the lake. He was training his much bigger kids in jiu-jitsu, a fighting technique focused on locking and holding opponents down to control them. The three friends agreed this technique was the best way to defend themselves from the predators.

They approached the old Siamese fish, Steve, to teach them jiu-jitsu. When Steve heard about the attack, he gladly agreed to teach all three.

Archer and his friends trained every day after school. The first few days were extremely painful, and they struggled a lot. Archer was getting locked up, choked, and beaten up by the much shorter and elder Steve.

But with hard work and discipline, they all became stronger and more confident. Steve was very proud of them. They were ready.

The day to showcase their new fighting technique had arrived. The predators were back. They chased all the other fish and started destroying homes again.

Archer, Dan, Georgia, and Steve confidently faced them. After seeing Archer, the predators laughed and reminded him of how helpless he was the last time they attacked.

The battle for the lake began. Everyone was amazed to see that the predators were getting defeated one by one. Jiu-jitsu complimented Archer's special abilities well. In no time, the predators were swimming away in fear. Archer and the team were able to drive them away for good. Everyone cheered them on.

In awe of Archer's bravery, everyone voiced their regret for having treated him horribly. They understood that his selflessness, courage, and special abilities were unique and should not be made fun of. All the fish in the lake started to respect and appreciate Archer. They even dubbed him the 'Guardian of the Lake.'

Archer had a happy and peaceful life, surrounded by loved ones who appreciated him for who he was. He eagerly anticipated going to school and jiu-jitsu training every day.

He put a lot of effort into achieving his dream of someday becoming the CEO of his own company. Archer felt he could accomplish anything he set his mind to with hard work and the help of everyone in his community.

Archer and the other axolotls are special creatures but also very endangered. This means few of them are left in the world. They only live in one place, in a unique lake in Mexico called Lake Xochimilco, which is their natural habitat. But unfortunately, humans have been hurting the axolotls' home by polluting the lake and building things around it. This makes it hard for the axolotls to survive.

But there is good news! We can help protect them by caring for the lake and their home. We can do things like not throwing trash in the lake or not using chemicals that can hurt the water. We can also ensure that we do not build structures too close to the lake so that the axolotls have a safe place to live. And if we ever see Archer or any other axolotl, we should be careful not to harm them and, instead, observe them from a distance.

By doing these things, we can help the axolotls survive and thrive in their natural habitat. That will make the lake a better place for them and for us!

www.ingramcontent.com/pod-product-compliance
Lightning Source LLC
Chambersburg PA
CBHW081630100526
44590CB00021B/3676